50 Sushi Bowl Recipes

By: Kelly Johnson

Table of Contents

- Classic California Roll Bowl
- Spicy Tuna Sushi Bowl
- Salmon Avocado Bowl
- Teriyaki Chicken Sushi Bowl
- Shrimp Tempura Bowl
- Rainbow Sushi Bowl
- Sashimi Tuna Bowl
- Veggie Sushi Bowl
- Eel Sauce Salmon Bowl
- Quinoa Sushi Bowl
- Poke Bowl with Ahi Tuna
- Miso Glazed Eggplant Bowl
- Crab and Avocado Bowl
- Shrimp and Mango Sushi Bowl
- Kimchi Sushi Bowl
- Spicy Salmon and Avocado Bowl
- Beet and Avocado Sushi Bowl
- Citrus Shrimp Bowl
- Tofu Teriyaki Bowl
- Chicken Katsu Sushi Bowl
- Asian Sesame Salad Bowl
- Salmon Poke Bowl with Seaweed
- Veggie Tempura Sushi Bowl
- Cilantro Lime Rice Bowl with Shrimp
- Spicy Scallop Sushi Bowl
- Coconut Rice Sushi Bowl
- Cucumber and Carrot Sushi Bowl
- Thai Peanut Chicken Sushi Bowl
- Grilled Vegetable Sushi Bowl
- Sashimi Salmon Bowl with Wasabi
- Egg and Spinach Sushi Bowl
- Avocado and Crab Sushi Bowl
- Teriyaki Tofu and Vegetable Bowl
- Spicy Tuna Poke Bowl
- Black Rice Sushi Bowl

- Salmon and Cream Cheese Bowl
- Sweet Potato Sushi Bowl
- Grilled Miso Cod Bowl
- Sesame Ginger Chicken Bowl
- Chilled Noodle Sushi Bowl
- Miso Soup Sushi Bowl
- Korean Beef Sushi Bowl
- Yakiniku Beef Bowl
- Sushi Bowl with Crunchy Garlic
- Vegetarian Sushi Bowl with Tofu
- Wasabi Shrimp Bowl
- Sweet Chili Chicken Bowl
- Tuna Tataki Bowl
- Seared Scallop Sushi Bowl
- Rainbow Veggie Sushi Bowl

Classic California Roll Bowl

Ingredients:

- 1 cup sushi rice
- 1 1/4 cups water
- 2 tablespoons rice vinegar
- 1 tablespoon sugar
- 1/2 teaspoon salt
- 1/2 avocado, sliced
- 1/2 cucumber, julienned
- 1/2 cup imitation crab meat, shredded
- Sesame seeds for garnish
- Nori sheets for serving

Instructions:

1. Rinse sushi rice under cold water until the water runs clear.
2. Combine rice and water in a rice cooker or pot, and cook according to package instructions.
3. In a small bowl, mix rice vinegar, sugar, and salt until dissolved.
4. Once rice is cooked, fluff with a fork and gently mix in the vinegar mixture.
5. To assemble, place rice in a bowl and top with avocado, cucumber, crab meat, and sesame seeds. Serve with nori sheets on the side.

Spicy Tuna Sushi Bowl

Ingredients:

- 1 cup sushi rice
- 1 1/4 cups water
- 1 tablespoon rice vinegar
- 1 tablespoon mayonnaise
- 1 teaspoon sriracha (adjust to taste)
- 1/2 pound sushi-grade tuna, diced
- 1/2 avocado, sliced
- 1/4 cucumber, julienned
- Green onions for garnish
- Sesame seeds for garnish

Instructions:

1. Rinse sushi rice under cold water until the water runs clear.
2. Combine rice and water in a rice cooker or pot, and cook according to package instructions.
3. In a bowl, mix rice vinegar, mayonnaise, and sriracha.
4. Once rice is cooked, fluff with a fork and gently mix in the vinegar mixture.
5. To assemble, place rice in a bowl and top with diced tuna, avocado, cucumber, green onions, and sesame seeds.

Salmon Avocado Bowl

Ingredients:

- 1 cup sushi rice
- 1 1/4 cups water
- 2 tablespoons rice vinegar
- 1/2 pound sushi-grade salmon, sliced
- 1/2 avocado, sliced
- 1/4 cup edamame, shelled
- 1/4 cup radishes, thinly sliced
- Soy sauce for drizzling
- Pickled ginger for garnish

Instructions:

1. Rinse sushi rice under cold water until the water runs clear.
2. Combine rice and water in a rice cooker or pot, and cook according to package instructions.
3. In a small bowl, mix rice vinegar with a pinch of salt.
4. Once rice is cooked, fluff with a fork and mix in the vinegar.
5. To assemble, place rice in a bowl and top with salmon, avocado, edamame, radishes, and drizzle with soy sauce. Garnish with pickled ginger.

Teriyaki Chicken Sushi Bowl

Ingredients:

- 1 cup sushi rice
- 1 1/4 cups water
- 1 tablespoon rice vinegar
- 1 cup cooked chicken, shredded
- 1/4 cup teriyaki sauce
- 1/2 avocado, sliced
- 1/4 cup carrot, shredded
- 1/4 cup cucumber, julienned
- Sesame seeds for garnish

Instructions:

1. Rinse sushi rice under cold water until the water runs clear.
2. Combine rice and water in a rice cooker or pot, and cook according to package instructions.
3. In a skillet, heat shredded chicken with teriyaki sauce until warmed through.
4. In a small bowl, mix rice vinegar with a pinch of salt.
5. Once rice is cooked, fluff with a fork and mix in the vinegar.
6. To assemble, place rice in a bowl and top with teriyaki chicken, avocado, carrot, cucumber, and sesame seeds.

Shrimp Tempura Bowl

Ingredients:

- 1 cup sushi rice
- 1 1/4 cups water
- 2 tablespoons rice vinegar
- 8-10 shrimp, peeled and deveined
- 1 cup tempura batter mix
- 1/2 cup ice-cold water
- Oil for frying
- 1/2 avocado, sliced
- 1/4 cup radishes, thinly sliced
- Soy sauce for drizzling

Instructions:

1. Rinse sushi rice under cold water until the water runs clear.
2. Combine rice and water in a rice cooker or pot, and cook according to package instructions.
3. In a bowl, mix tempura batter with ice-cold water until smooth.
4. Heat oil in a deep skillet. Dip shrimp in the batter and fry until golden brown.
5. In a small bowl, mix rice vinegar with a pinch of salt.
6. Once rice is cooked, fluff with a fork and mix in the vinegar.
7. To assemble, place rice in a bowl and top with shrimp tempura, avocado, radishes, and drizzle with soy sauce.

Rainbow Sushi Bowl

Ingredients:

- 1 cup sushi rice
- 1 1/4 cups water
- 2 tablespoons rice vinegar
- 1/2 pound mixed sushi-grade fish (salmon, tuna, yellowtail), sliced
- 1/2 avocado, sliced
- 1/2 cup cucumber, julienned
- 1/4 cup radishes, thinly sliced
- Seaweed salad for garnish
- Soy sauce for drizzling

Instructions:

1. Rinse sushi rice under cold water until the water runs clear.
2. Combine rice and water in a rice cooker or pot, and cook according to package instructions.
3. In a small bowl, mix rice vinegar with a pinch of salt.
4. Once rice is cooked, fluff with a fork and mix in the vinegar.
5. To assemble, place rice in a bowl and arrange mixed fish, avocado, cucumber, radishes, and seaweed salad on top. Drizzle with soy sauce.

Sashimi Tuna Bowl

Ingredients:

- 1 cup sushi rice
- 1 1/4 cups water
- 2 tablespoons rice vinegar
- 1/2 pound sushi-grade tuna, sliced
- 1/2 avocado, sliced
- 1/4 cup cucumber, julienned
- Wasabi and pickled ginger for serving
- Soy sauce for drizzling

Instructions:

1. Rinse sushi rice under cold water until the water runs clear.
2. Combine rice and water in a rice cooker or pot, and cook according to package instructions.
3. In a small bowl, mix rice vinegar with a pinch of salt.
4. Once rice is cooked, fluff with a fork and mix in the vinegar.
5. To assemble, place rice in a bowl and top with sashimi tuna, avocado, cucumber, and drizzle with soy sauce. Serve with wasabi and pickled ginger.

Veggie Sushi Bowl

Ingredients:

- 1 cup sushi rice
- 1 1/4 cups water
- 2 tablespoons rice vinegar
- 1/4 cup carrot, julienned
- 1/4 cup cucumber, julienned
- 1/4 cup bell pepper, sliced
- 1/4 cup radishes, thinly sliced
- 1/2 avocado, sliced
- Sesame seeds for garnish
- Soy sauce for drizzling

Instructions:

1. Rinse sushi rice under cold water until the water runs clear.
2. Combine rice and water in a rice cooker or pot, and cook according to package instructions.
3. In a small bowl, mix rice vinegar with a pinch of salt.
4. Once rice is cooked, fluff with a fork and mix in the vinegar.
5. To assemble, place rice in a bowl and top with carrot, cucumber, bell pepper, radishes, avocado, and sesame seeds. Drizzle with soy sauce.

Eel Sauce Salmon Bowl

Ingredients:

- 1 cup sushi rice
- 1 1/4 cups water
- 2 tablespoons rice vinegar
- 1/2 pound sushi-grade salmon, sliced
- 1/4 cup eel sauce
- 1/2 avocado, sliced
- 1/4 cup cucumber, julienned
- Sesame seeds for garnish

Instructions:

1. Rinse sushi rice under cold water until the water runs clear.
2. Combine rice and water in a rice cooker or pot, and cook according to package instructions.
3. In a small bowl, mix rice vinegar with a pinch of salt.
4. Once rice is cooked, fluff with a fork and mix in the vinegar.
5. To assemble, place rice in a bowl and top with salmon, eel sauce, avocado, cucumber, and sesame seeds.

Quinoa Sushi Bowl

Ingredients:

- 1 cup quinoa
- 2 cups water
- 2 tablespoons rice vinegar
- 1/2 avocado, sliced
- 1/2 cucumber, julienned
- 1/4 cup shredded carrots
- 1/2 cup edamame, shelled
- Nori sheets for serving
- Soy sauce for drizzling

Instructions:

1. Rinse quinoa under cold water until the water runs clear.
2. Combine quinoa and water in a pot, bring to a boil, then reduce heat and simmer until quinoa is cooked (about 15 minutes).
3. In a small bowl, mix rice vinegar with a pinch of salt.
4. Once quinoa is cooked, fluff with a fork and mix in the vinegar.
5. To assemble, place quinoa in a bowl and top with avocado, cucumber, carrots, edamame, and drizzle with soy sauce. Serve with nori sheets on the side.

Poke Bowl with Ahi Tuna

Ingredients:

- 1 cup sushi rice
- 1 1/4 cups water
- 2 tablespoons rice vinegar
- 1/2 pound sushi-grade ahi tuna, cubed
- 1 tablespoon soy sauce
- 1 teaspoon sesame oil
- 1/2 avocado, sliced
- 1/4 cup cucumber, sliced
- Green onions for garnish
- Sesame seeds for garnish

Instructions:

1. Rinse sushi rice under cold water until the water runs clear.
2. Combine rice and water in a rice cooker or pot, and cook according to package instructions.
3. In a bowl, mix soy sauce and sesame oil, and marinate the tuna cubes for 10 minutes.
4. In a small bowl, mix rice vinegar with a pinch of salt.
5. Once rice is cooked, fluff with a fork and mix in the vinegar.
6. To assemble, place rice in a bowl and top with marinated tuna, avocado, cucumber, green onions, and sesame seeds.

Miso Glazed Eggplant Bowl

Ingredients:

- 1 cup sushi rice
- 1 1/4 cups water
- 2 tablespoons rice vinegar
- 1 large eggplant, sliced
- 2 tablespoons miso paste
- 1 tablespoon honey
- 1 tablespoon soy sauce
- 1/2 avocado, sliced
- 1/4 cup scallions, chopped
- Sesame seeds for garnish

Instructions:

1. Rinse sushi rice under cold water until the water runs clear.
2. Combine rice and water in a rice cooker or pot, and cook according to package instructions.
3. In a small bowl, mix miso paste, honey, and soy sauce.
4. Preheat the oven to 400°F (200°C). Brush eggplant slices with the miso mixture and roast for 20 minutes or until tender.
5. In a small bowl, mix rice vinegar with a pinch of salt.
6. Once rice is cooked, fluff with a fork and mix in the vinegar.
7. To assemble, place rice in a bowl and top with miso-glazed eggplant, avocado, scallions, and sesame seeds.

Crab and Avocado Bowl

Ingredients:

- 1 cup sushi rice
- 1 1/4 cups water
- 2 tablespoons rice vinegar
- 1 cup cooked crab meat
- 1/2 avocado, sliced
- 1/4 cup cucumber, julienned
- 1/4 cup carrots, shredded
- Soy sauce for drizzling
- Sesame seeds for garnish

Instructions:

1. Rinse sushi rice under cold water until the water runs clear.
2. Combine rice and water in a rice cooker or pot, and cook according to package instructions.
3. In a small bowl, mix rice vinegar with a pinch of salt.
4. Once rice is cooked, fluff with a fork and mix in the vinegar.
5. To assemble, place rice in a bowl and top with crab meat, avocado, cucumber, carrots, and drizzle with soy sauce. Garnish with sesame seeds.

Shrimp and Mango Sushi Bowl

Ingredients:

- 1 cup sushi rice
- 1 1/4 cups water
- 2 tablespoons rice vinegar
- 1/2 pound cooked shrimp, peeled and deveined
- 1/2 mango, diced
- 1/2 avocado, sliced
- 1/4 cup cucumber, julienned
- Lime wedges for serving
- Cilantro for garnish

Instructions:

1. Rinse sushi rice under cold water until the water runs clear.
2. Combine rice and water in a rice cooker or pot, and cook according to package instructions.
3. In a small bowl, mix rice vinegar with a pinch of salt.
4. Once rice is cooked, fluff with a fork and mix in the vinegar.
5. To assemble, place rice in a bowl and top with shrimp, mango, avocado, cucumber, and garnish with cilantro. Serve with lime wedges.

Kimchi Sushi Bowl

Ingredients:

- 1 cup sushi rice
- 1 1/4 cups water
- 2 tablespoons rice vinegar
- 1/2 cup kimchi, chopped
- 1/2 avocado, sliced
- 1/4 cup radishes, thinly sliced
- Green onions for garnish
- Sesame seeds for garnish

Instructions:

1. Rinse sushi rice under cold water until the water runs clear.
2. Combine rice and water in a rice cooker or pot, and cook according to package instructions.
3. In a small bowl, mix rice vinegar with a pinch of salt.
4. Once rice is cooked, fluff with a fork and mix in the vinegar.
5. To assemble, place rice in a bowl and top with kimchi, avocado, radishes, green onions, and sesame seeds.

Spicy Salmon and Avocado Bowl

Ingredients:

- 1 cup sushi rice
- 1 1/4 cups water
- 2 tablespoons rice vinegar
- 1/2 pound sushi-grade salmon, cubed
- 1 tablespoon sriracha (adjust to taste)
- 1/2 avocado, sliced
- 1/4 cup cucumber, sliced
- Seaweed salad for garnish
- Soy sauce for drizzling

Instructions:

1. Rinse sushi rice under cold water until the water runs clear.
2. Combine rice and water in a rice cooker or pot, and cook according to package instructions.
3. In a bowl, mix salmon with sriracha.
4. In a small bowl, mix rice vinegar with a pinch of salt.
5. Once rice is cooked, fluff with a fork and mix in the vinegar.
6. To assemble, place rice in a bowl and top with spicy salmon, avocado, cucumber, and garnish with seaweed salad. Drizzle with soy sauce.

Beet and Avocado Sushi Bowl

Ingredients:

- 1 cup sushi rice
- 1 1/4 cups water
- 2 tablespoons rice vinegar
- 1 medium beet, roasted and diced
- 1/2 avocado, sliced
- 1/4 cup cucumber, sliced
- 1/4 cup goat cheese, crumbled
- Walnuts for garnish
- Balsamic glaze for drizzling

Instructions:

1. Rinse sushi rice under cold water until the water runs clear.
2. Combine rice and water in a rice cooker or pot, and cook according to package instructions.
3. In a small bowl, mix rice vinegar with a pinch of salt.
4. Once rice is cooked, fluff with a fork and mix in the vinegar.
5. To assemble, place rice in a bowl and top with roasted beet, avocado, cucumber, goat cheese, and walnuts. Drizzle with balsamic glaze.

Citrus Shrimp Bowl

Ingredients:

- 1 cup jasmine rice
- 1 1/4 cups water
- 1 pound shrimp, peeled and deveined
- Zest and juice of 1 orange
- Zest and juice of 1 lime
- 1 tablespoon olive oil
- 1 avocado, sliced
- 1/4 cup cilantro, chopped
- Salt and pepper to taste

Instructions:

1. Rinse jasmine rice under cold water until the water runs clear.
2. Combine rice and water in a pot, bring to a boil, then reduce heat and simmer until rice is cooked (about 15 minutes).
3. In a bowl, mix olive oil, orange zest, lime zest, orange juice, lime juice, salt, and pepper.
4. Marinate shrimp in the citrus mixture for 15 minutes.
5. Sauté shrimp in a skillet over medium heat until cooked through (about 3-4 minutes).
6. To assemble, place rice in a bowl and top with citrus shrimp, avocado, and cilantro.

Tofu Teriyaki Bowl

Ingredients:

- 1 cup brown rice
- 1 1/4 cups water
- 1 block firm tofu, cubed
- 1/4 cup teriyaki sauce
- 1 cup broccoli florets
- 1/2 bell pepper, sliced
- 1 tablespoon sesame oil
- Green onions for garnish
- Sesame seeds for garnish

Instructions:

1. Rinse brown rice under cold water until the water runs clear.
2. Combine rice and water in a pot, bring to a boil, then reduce heat and simmer until rice is cooked (about 45 minutes).
3. In a skillet, heat sesame oil and sauté tofu until golden brown (about 5 minutes).
4. Add broccoli and bell pepper, and cook until tender (about 3-4 minutes).
5. Stir in teriyaki sauce and cook for another 2 minutes.
6. To assemble, place rice in a bowl and top with tofu teriyaki mix, and garnish with green onions and sesame seeds.

Chicken Katsu Sushi Bowl

Ingredients:

- 1 cup sushi rice
- 1 1/4 cups water
- 2 chicken breasts
- 1/2 cup panko breadcrumbs
- 1/4 cup flour
- 1 egg, beaten
- 1/4 cup tonkatsu sauce
- 1/2 avocado, sliced
- 1/4 cup cucumber, sliced
- Pickled ginger for serving

Instructions:

1. Rinse sushi rice under cold water until the water runs clear.
2. Combine rice and water in a rice cooker or pot, and cook according to package instructions.
3. Dredge chicken breasts in flour, dip in beaten egg, and coat with panko breadcrumbs.
4. Heat oil in a skillet and fry chicken until golden brown and cooked through (about 5-6 minutes per side).
5. Once rice is cooked, fluff with a fork and mix in vinegar.
6. To assemble, place rice in a bowl and top with sliced chicken katsu, tonkatsu sauce, avocado, cucumber, and pickled ginger.

Asian Sesame Salad Bowl

Ingredients:

- 4 cups mixed salad greens
- 1 cup shredded carrots
- 1 cup cucumber, sliced
- 1/2 cup edamame, shelled
- 1/4 cup sliced almonds
- 1/4 cup sesame dressing
- 1 tablespoon sesame seeds

Instructions:

1. In a large bowl, combine salad greens, shredded carrots, cucumber, and edamame.
2. Drizzle with sesame dressing and toss to combine.
3. Top with sliced almonds and sprinkle with sesame seeds.
4. Serve immediately as a refreshing salad bowl.

Salmon Poke Bowl with Seaweed

Ingredients:

- 1 cup sushi rice
- 1 1/4 cups water
- 1/2 pound sushi-grade salmon, cubed
- 1 tablespoon soy sauce
- 1 teaspoon sesame oil
- 1/2 avocado, sliced
- 1/4 cup seaweed salad
- 1/4 cup cucumber, sliced
- Green onions for garnish
- Sesame seeds for garnish

Instructions:

1. Rinse sushi rice under cold water until the water runs clear.
2. Combine rice and water in a rice cooker or pot, and cook according to package instructions.
3. In a bowl, mix salmon with soy sauce and sesame oil.
4. Once rice is cooked, fluff with a fork and mix in rice vinegar.
5. To assemble, place rice in a bowl and top with salmon, avocado, seaweed salad, cucumber, and garnish with green onions and sesame seeds.

Veggie Tempura Sushi Bowl

Ingredients:

- 1 cup sushi rice
- 1 1/4 cups water
- 1 zucchini, sliced
- 1 sweet potato, peeled and sliced
- 1/2 cup tempura batter mix
- 1 cup cold water
- Vegetable oil for frying
- 1/4 cup soy sauce
- 1/2 avocado, sliced
- Sesame seeds for garnish

Instructions:

1. Rinse sushi rice under cold water until the water runs clear.
2. Combine rice and water in a rice cooker or pot, and cook according to package instructions.
3. Prepare tempura batter by mixing tempura batter mix with cold water until smooth.
4. Heat oil in a deep pan and dip vegetables in batter, then fry until golden brown (about 3-4 minutes).
5. Once rice is cooked, fluff with a fork and mix in rice vinegar.
6. To assemble, place rice in a bowl and top with tempura veggies, avocado, and drizzle with soy sauce. Garnish with sesame seeds.

Cilantro Lime Rice Bowl with Shrimp

Ingredients:

- 1 cup jasmine rice
- 1 1/4 cups water
- 1 pound shrimp, peeled and deveined
- Zest and juice of 1 lime
- 1/4 cup cilantro, chopped
- 1 tablespoon olive oil
- 1/2 cup black beans
- 1/2 avocado, sliced
- Salt and pepper to taste

Instructions:

1. Rinse jasmine rice under cold water until the water runs clear.
2. Combine rice and water in a pot, bring to a boil, then reduce heat and simmer until rice is cooked (about 15 minutes).
3. In a bowl, mix olive oil, lime zest, lime juice, salt, and pepper.
4. Marinate shrimp in the lime mixture for 15 minutes.
5. Sauté shrimp in a skillet over medium heat until cooked through (about 3-4 minutes).
6. Once rice is cooked, fluff with a fork and mix in cilantro.
7. To assemble, place cilantro lime rice in a bowl and top with shrimp, black beans, and avocado.

Spicy Scallop Sushi Bowl

Ingredients:

- 1 cup sushi rice
- 1 1/4 cups water
- 1/2 pound scallops, cleaned
- 1 tablespoon sriracha
- 1 tablespoon soy sauce
- 1/2 avocado, sliced
- 1/4 cup cucumber, sliced
- Seaweed salad for garnish
- Sesame seeds for garnish

Instructions:

1. Rinse sushi rice under cold water until the water runs clear.
2. Combine rice and water in a rice cooker or pot, and cook according to package instructions.
3. In a bowl, mix scallops with sriracha and soy sauce.
4. Sauté scallops in a skillet over medium heat until cooked through (about 2-3 minutes per side).
5. Once rice is cooked, fluff with a fork and mix in rice vinegar.
6. To assemble, place rice in a bowl and top with scallops, avocado, cucumber, and garnish with seaweed salad and sesame seeds.

Coconut Rice Sushi Bowl

Ingredients:

- 1 cup jasmine rice
- 1 can (13.5 oz) coconut milk
- 1/2 cup water
- 1/4 cup shredded coconut
- 1/2 pound shrimp, peeled and deveined
- 1 tablespoon lime juice
- 1/2 avocado, sliced
- Cilantro for garnish

Instructions:

1. Rinse jasmine rice under cold water until the water runs clear.
2. In a pot, combine rice, coconut milk, and water. Bring to a boil, then reduce heat and simmer until rice is cooked (about 15 minutes).
3. In a bowl, marinate shrimp in lime juice for 10 minutes.
4. Sauté shrimp in a skillet over medium heat until cooked through (about 3-4 minutes).
5. Once rice is cooked, fluff with a fork and mix in shredded coconut.
6. To assemble, place coconut rice in a bowl and top with shrimp, avocado, and garnish with cilantro.

Cucumber and Carrot Sushi Bowl

Ingredients:

- 1 cup sushi rice
- 1 1/4 cups water
- 1 cucumber, julienned
- 1 carrot, julienned
- 1 avocado, sliced
- 1/4 cup rice vinegar
- 1 tablespoon soy sauce
- Sesame seeds for garnish

Instructions:

1. Rinse sushi rice under cold water until the water runs clear.
2. Combine rice and water in a rice cooker or pot, and cook according to package instructions.
3. Once rice is cooked, fluff with a fork and mix in rice vinegar.
4. To assemble, place rice in a bowl and top with cucumber, carrot, and avocado. Drizzle with soy sauce and garnish with sesame seeds.

Thai Peanut Chicken Sushi Bowl

Ingredients:

- 1 cup jasmine rice
- 1 1/4 cups water
- 1 cup cooked chicken, shredded
- 1/4 cup peanut sauce
- 1/2 red bell pepper, sliced
- 1/2 cup snap peas
- Chopped peanuts for garnish
- Cilantro for garnish

Instructions:

1. Rinse jasmine rice under cold water until the water runs clear.
2. Combine rice and water in a pot, bring to a boil, then reduce heat and simmer until rice is cooked (about 15 minutes).
3. In a bowl, combine cooked chicken with peanut sauce until well coated.
4. Once rice is cooked, fluff with a fork and add to a bowl.
5. Top with chicken mixture, red bell pepper, and snap peas. Garnish with chopped peanuts and cilantro.

Grilled Vegetable Sushi Bowl

Ingredients:

- 1 cup sushi rice
- 1 1/4 cups water
- 1 zucchini, sliced
- 1 bell pepper, sliced
- 1 eggplant, sliced
- 1 tablespoon olive oil
- 2 tablespoons balsamic vinegar
- 1/4 cup hummus
- Fresh basil for garnish

Instructions:

1. Rinse sushi rice under cold water until the water runs clear.
2. Combine rice and water in a rice cooker or pot, and cook according to package instructions.
3. Toss zucchini, bell pepper, and eggplant with olive oil and balsamic vinegar. Grill until tender.
4. Once rice is cooked, fluff with a fork.
5. To assemble, place rice in a bowl and top with grilled vegetables and a dollop of hummus. Garnish with fresh basil.

Sashimi Salmon Bowl with Wasabi

Ingredients:

- 1 cup sushi rice
- 1 1/4 cups water
- 1/2 pound sushi-grade salmon, sliced
- 1 tablespoon soy sauce
- 1 teaspoon wasabi
- 1/2 avocado, sliced
- Seaweed salad for garnish
- Sesame seeds for garnish

Instructions:

1. Rinse sushi rice under cold water until the water runs clear.
2. Combine rice and water in a rice cooker or pot, and cook according to package instructions.
3. Once rice is cooked, fluff with a fork and mix in rice vinegar.
4. To assemble, place rice in a bowl and top with salmon slices, avocado, and a side of wasabi. Garnish with seaweed salad and sesame seeds.

Egg and Spinach Sushi Bowl

Ingredients:

- 1 cup sushi rice
- 1 1/4 cups water
- 4 eggs, beaten
- 2 cups spinach, sautéed
- 1 tablespoon soy sauce
- Sesame seeds for garnish

Instructions:

1. Rinse sushi rice under cold water until the water runs clear.
2. Combine rice and water in a rice cooker or pot, and cook according to package instructions.
3. In a skillet, scramble the beaten eggs until fully cooked.
4. Once rice is cooked, fluff with a fork and mix in rice vinegar.
5. To assemble, place rice in a bowl and top with scrambled eggs and sautéed spinach. Drizzle with soy sauce and sprinkle with sesame seeds.

Avocado and Crab Sushi Bowl

Ingredients:

- 1 cup sushi rice
- 1 1/4 cups water
- 1/2 pound imitation crab meat, shredded
- 1 avocado, sliced
- 1 tablespoon mayonnaise
- 1 tablespoon soy sauce
- 1/4 cup cucumber, diced
- Sesame seeds for garnish

Instructions:

1. Rinse sushi rice under cold water until the water runs clear.
2. Combine rice and water in a rice cooker or pot, and cook according to package instructions.
3. In a bowl, mix shredded crab meat with mayonnaise and soy sauce.
4. Once rice is cooked, fluff with a fork and mix in rice vinegar.
5. To assemble, place rice in a bowl and top with crab mixture, avocado, and diced cucumber. Garnish with sesame seeds.

Teriyaki Tofu and Vegetable Bowl

Ingredients:

- 1 cup brown rice
- 1 1/4 cups water
- 1 block firm tofu, cubed
- 1 cup mixed vegetables (bell peppers, broccoli, carrots)
- 1/4 cup teriyaki sauce
- 1 tablespoon sesame oil
- Green onions for garnish
- Sesame seeds for garnish

Instructions:

1. Rinse brown rice under cold water until the water runs clear.
2. Combine rice and water in a pot, bring to a boil, then reduce heat and simmer until rice is cooked (about 45 minutes).
3. In a skillet, heat sesame oil and sauté tofu until golden brown.
4. Add mixed vegetables and stir in teriyaki sauce, cooking until vegetables are tender.
5. Once rice is cooked, fluff with a fork.
6. To assemble, place rice in a bowl and top with tofu and vegetable mixture. Garnish with green onions and sesame seeds.

Spicy Tuna Poke Bowl

Ingredients:

- 1 cup sushi rice
- 1 1/4 cups water
- 1/2 pound sushi-grade tuna, cubed
- 1 tablespoon sriracha
- 1 tablespoon soy sauce
- 1/2 avocado, sliced
- 1/4 cup cucumber, diced
- Seaweed salad for garnish
- Sesame seeds for garnish

Instructions:

1. Rinse sushi rice under cold water until the water runs clear.
2. Combine rice and water in a rice cooker or pot, and cook according to package instructions.
3. In a bowl, mix tuna with sriracha and soy sauce.
4. Once rice is cooked, fluff with a fork and mix in rice vinegar.
5. To assemble, place rice in a bowl and top with spicy tuna, avocado, cucumber, and garnish with seaweed salad and sesame seeds.

Black Rice Sushi Bowl

Ingredients:

- 1 cup black rice
- 1 3/4 cups water
- 1/2 cucumber, diced
- 1/2 avocado, sliced
- 1/2 cup edamame, shelled
- 1/4 cup carrots, julienned
- 2 tablespoons rice vinegar
- 1 tablespoon soy sauce
- Sesame seeds for garnish

Instructions:

1. Rinse black rice under cold water until the water runs clear.
2. Combine rice and water in a pot, bring to a boil, then reduce heat and simmer until rice is cooked (about 30-40 minutes).
3. Once rice is cooked, fluff with a fork and mix in rice vinegar.
4. To assemble, place rice in a bowl and top with cucumber, avocado, edamame, and carrots. Drizzle with soy sauce and garnish with sesame seeds.

Salmon and Cream Cheese Bowl

Ingredients:

- 1 cup sushi rice
- 1 1/4 cups water
- 1/2 pound sushi-grade salmon, sliced
- 1/4 cup cream cheese, softened
- 1 tablespoon chives, chopped
- 1/4 avocado, sliced
- 1/4 cup cucumber, sliced
- Soy sauce for drizzling

Instructions:

1. Rinse sushi rice under cold water until the water runs clear.
2. Combine rice and water in a rice cooker or pot, and cook according to package instructions.
3. Once rice is cooked, fluff with a fork and mix in rice vinegar.
4. To assemble, place rice in a bowl and layer with salmon slices, cream cheese, chives, avocado, and cucumber. Drizzle with soy sauce.

Sweet Potato Sushi Bowl

Ingredients:

- 1 cup sushi rice
- 1 1/4 cups water
- 1 medium sweet potato, roasted and diced
- 1/2 avocado, sliced
- 1/4 cup cucumber, diced
- 2 tablespoons tahini
- 1 tablespoon soy sauce
- Sesame seeds for garnish

Instructions:

1. Rinse sushi rice under cold water until the water runs clear.
2. Combine rice and water in a rice cooker or pot, and cook according to package instructions.
3. Once rice is cooked, fluff with a fork and mix in rice vinegar.
4. To assemble, place rice in a bowl and top with roasted sweet potato, avocado, cucumber, tahini, and a drizzle of soy sauce. Garnish with sesame seeds.

Grilled Miso Cod Bowl

Ingredients:

- 1 cup sushi rice
- 1 1/4 cups water
- 2 miso-marinated cod fillets
- 1/2 cup snap peas
- 1/4 cup carrot, julienned
- 2 tablespoons soy sauce
- Green onions for garnish

Instructions:

1. Rinse sushi rice under cold water until the water runs clear.
2. Combine rice and water in a rice cooker or pot, and cook according to package instructions.
3. Grill or pan-sear the miso-marinated cod until cooked through.
4. Blanch snap peas and carrots in boiling water for 1-2 minutes, then cool in ice water.
5. To assemble, place rice in a bowl and top with grilled cod, snap peas, and carrots. Drizzle with soy sauce and garnish with green onions.

Sesame Ginger Chicken Bowl

Ingredients:

- 1 cup brown rice
- 1 1/4 cups water
- 1 cup cooked chicken, shredded
- 2 tablespoons sesame oil
- 1 tablespoon ginger, minced
- 1/4 cup soy sauce
- 1/2 cup broccoli florets
- Sesame seeds for garnish

Instructions:

1. Rinse brown rice under cold water until the water runs clear.
2. Combine rice and water in a pot, bring to a boil, then reduce heat and simmer until rice is cooked (about 45 minutes).
3. In a skillet, heat sesame oil and sauté ginger.
4. Add shredded chicken and soy sauce, cooking until heated through.
5. Steam broccoli until tender.
6. To assemble, place rice in a bowl and top with chicken mixture, broccoli, and sprinkle with sesame seeds.

Chilled Noodle Sushi Bowl

Ingredients:

- 1 cup soba noodles
- 1 1/4 cups water
- 1/2 cucumber, julienned
- 1/2 carrot, julienned
- 1/4 cup edamame, shelled
- 2 tablespoons sesame dressing
- 1 tablespoon soy sauce
- Sesame seeds for garnish

Instructions:

1. Cook soba noodles according to package instructions and rinse under cold water to cool.
2. Once cooled, toss noodles with sesame dressing and soy sauce.
3. To assemble, place noodles in a bowl and top with cucumber, carrot, and edamame. Garnish with sesame seeds.

Miso Soup Sushi Bowl

Ingredients:

- 1 cup sushi rice
- 1 1/4 cups water
- 1/4 cup miso paste
- 4 cups water (for soup)
- 1/2 cup tofu, cubed
- 1/4 cup green onions, sliced
- 1 cup spinach

Instructions:

1. Rinse sushi rice under cold water until the water runs clear.
2. Combine rice and water in a rice cooker or pot, and cook according to package instructions.
3. In a separate pot, bring 4 cups of water to a boil, add miso paste, and stir until dissolved.
4. Add tofu and spinach, cooking until heated through.
5. Once rice is cooked, fluff with a fork.
6. To assemble, place rice in a bowl and pour miso soup over it, garnishing with green onions.

Korean Beef Sushi Bowl

Ingredients:

- 1 cup sushi rice
- 1 1/4 cups water
- 1/2 pound ground beef
- 2 tablespoons gochujang (Korean chili paste)
- 1 tablespoon soy sauce
- 1/4 cup carrots, shredded
- 1/4 cup cucumber, sliced
- Sesame seeds for garnish

Instructions:

1. Rinse sushi rice under cold water until the water runs clear.
2. Combine rice and water in a rice cooker or pot, and cook according to package instructions.
3. In a skillet, cook ground beef until browned, then mix in gochujang and soy sauce.
4. Once rice is cooked, fluff with a fork.
5. To assemble, place rice in a bowl and top with Korean beef, shredded carrots, and cucumber. Garnish with sesame seeds.

Yakiniku Beef Bowl

Ingredients:

- 1 cup sushi rice
- 1 1/4 cups water
- 1/2 pound beef, thinly sliced
- 2 tablespoons yakiniku sauce
- 1/4 cup green onions, chopped
- 1/2 cup mushrooms, sliced
- Sesame seeds for garnish

Instructions:

1. Rinse sushi rice under cold water until the water runs clear.
2. Combine rice and water in a rice cooker or pot, and cook according to package instructions.
3. In a skillet, cook beef and mushrooms over medium heat until browned.
4. Add yakiniku sauce and cook for another 2-3 minutes.
5. Once rice is cooked, fluff with a fork.
6. To assemble, place rice in a bowl and top with beef, mushrooms, and green onions. Garnish with sesame seeds.

Sushi Bowl with Crunchy Garlic

Ingredients:

- 1 cup sushi rice
- 1 1/4 cups water
- 1/2 cup cooked shrimp
- 2 tablespoons crunchy garlic (fried garlic)
- 1/2 cucumber, diced
- 1 avocado, sliced
- Soy sauce for drizzling

Instructions:

1. Rinse sushi rice under cold water until the water runs clear.
2. Combine rice and water in a rice cooker or pot, and cook according to package instructions.
3. Once rice is cooked, fluff with a fork and let it cool slightly.
4. To assemble, place rice in a bowl and top with shrimp, crunchy garlic, cucumber, and avocado. Drizzle with soy sauce.

Vegetarian Sushi Bowl with Tofu

Ingredients:

- 1 cup sushi rice
- 1 1/4 cups water
- 1/2 block firm tofu, cubed
- 1 tablespoon soy sauce
- 1/2 avocado, sliced
- 1/2 cup carrots, julienned
- 1/4 cup edamame, shelled
- Sesame seeds for garnish

Instructions:

1. Rinse sushi rice under cold water until the water runs clear.
2. Combine rice and water in a rice cooker or pot, and cook according to package instructions.
3. Sauté cubed tofu in a skillet until golden brown; add soy sauce and cook for another minute.
4. Once rice is cooked, fluff with a fork.
5. To assemble, place rice in a bowl and top with tofu, avocado, carrots, and edamame. Garnish with sesame seeds.

Wasabi Shrimp Bowl

Ingredients:

- 1 cup sushi rice
- 1 1/4 cups water
- 1/2 pound shrimp, peeled and deveined
- 1 tablespoon wasabi paste
- 2 tablespoons soy sauce
- 1/4 cup green onions, chopped
- 1/2 avocado, sliced

Instructions:

1. Rinse sushi rice under cold water until the water runs clear.
2. Combine rice and water in a rice cooker or pot, and cook according to package instructions.
3. Sauté shrimp in a skillet over medium heat until pink; mix in wasabi paste and soy sauce.
4. Once rice is cooked, fluff with a fork.
5. To assemble, place rice in a bowl and top with wasabi shrimp, green onions, and avocado.

Sweet Chili Chicken Bowl

Ingredients:

- 1 cup brown rice
- 1 1/4 cups water
- 1 pound chicken breast, cooked and shredded
- 1/4 cup sweet chili sauce
- 1/2 cup bell peppers, sliced
- 1/4 cup green onions, chopped
- Sesame seeds for garnish

Instructions:

1. Rinse brown rice under cold water until the water runs clear.
2. Combine rice and water in a pot, bring to a boil, then reduce heat and simmer until rice is cooked (about 45 minutes).
3. Mix shredded chicken with sweet chili sauce in a skillet and heat through.
4. Once rice is cooked, fluff with a fork.
5. To assemble, place rice in a bowl and top with sweet chili chicken, bell peppers, and green onions. Garnish with sesame seeds.

Tuna Tataki Bowl

Ingredients:

- 1 cup sushi rice
- 1 1/4 cups water
- 1/2 pound sushi-grade tuna, seared and sliced
- 2 tablespoons ponzu sauce
- 1/4 cup radish, thinly sliced
- 1/4 cup cucumber, sliced
- 1 tablespoon sesame seeds for garnish

Instructions:

1. Rinse sushi rice under cold water until the water runs clear.
2. Combine rice and water in a rice cooker or pot, and cook according to package instructions.
3. Once rice is cooked, fluff with a fork and let it cool slightly.
4. To assemble, place rice in a bowl and top with sliced tuna, ponzu sauce, radish, and cucumber. Garnish with sesame seeds.

Seared Scallop Sushi Bowl

Ingredients:

- 1 cup sushi rice
- 1 1/4 cups water
- 1/2 pound scallops, cleaned
- 1 tablespoon olive oil
- 2 tablespoons soy sauce
- 1/4 cup green onions, chopped
- 1/2 avocado, sliced

Instructions:

1. Rinse sushi rice under cold water until the water runs clear.
2. Combine rice and water in a rice cooker or pot, and cook according to package instructions.
3. Sear scallops in a skillet with olive oil over medium-high heat until golden brown on both sides.
4. Once rice is cooked, fluff with a fork.
5. To assemble, place rice in a bowl and top with seared scallops, soy sauce, green onions, and avocado.

Rainbow Veggie Sushi Bowl

Ingredients:

- 1 cup sushi rice
- 1 1/4 cups water
- 1/2 avocado, sliced
- 1/2 cucumber, diced
- 1/2 carrot, julienned
- 1/4 cup bell peppers, sliced
- 1/4 cup radishes, thinly sliced
- Soy sauce for drizzling

Instructions:

1. Rinse sushi rice under cold water until the water runs clear.
2. Combine rice and water in a rice cooker or pot, and cook according to package instructions.
3. Once rice is cooked, fluff with a fork.
4. To assemble, place rice in a bowl and top with avocado, cucumber, carrot, bell peppers, and radishes. Drizzle with soy sauce.